SOARING HIGH
LIKE
EAGLES

SOARING HIGH
LIKE
EAGLES

THE PEOPLE THAT WAIT ON GOD

STEPHEN IFEKOYA

authorHOUSE®

AuthorHouse™
1663 Liberty Drive
Bloomington, IN 47403
www.authorhouse.com
Phone: 1-800-839-8640

Published by AuthorHouse   04/04/2013

ISBN: 978-1-4817-8902-8 (sc)
ISBN: 978-1-4817-8903-5 (e)

Any people depicted in stock imagery provided by Thinkstock are models,
and such images are being used for illustrative purposes only.
Certain stock imagery © Thinkstock.

This book is printed on acid-free paper.

Because of the dynamic nature of the Internet, any web addresses or links
contained in this book may have changed since publication and may no longer be
valid. The views expressed in this work are solely those of the author and do not
necessarily reflect the views of the publisher, and the publisher hereby disclaims any
responsibility for them.

DEDICATION

I dedicate this book to the Trinity God: the Father,
the Son and the Holy Spirit

CONTENTS

Acknowledgments

First and foremost, I want to give thanks to God for bringing this dream to pass. Many have died without fulfilling their dreams but by His grace this has come to reality.

I must thank God for my wife and our children for their unfailing support that have enabled me to bring this dream to fruition. They are more precious to me than silver and gold.

I must thank God for bringing Tshipi Alexander at the fullness of time to support the publishing of this book, morally and financially. I pray that God will bless him and his family greatly.

I give thanks to God for my mentors in ministry, colleagues, friends, my siblings and my wife's family that have added value to my life at various times.

Finally, I must appreciate Maria Anderson for her restless effort to convince me that it is time to bring this dream to reality. I must also express my appreciation to all the staff of AuthorHouse publishers, U.K.

INTRODUCTION

I am the true vine, and my Father is the
husbandman.

Every branch in me that beareth not
fruit he taketh away: and every branch
that beareth fruit, he purgeth it, that it
may bring forth more fruit.

Now ye are clean through the word
which I have spoken unto you.

Abide in me, and I in you. As the
branch cannot bear fruit of itself, except
it abide in the vine; no more can ye,
except ye abide in me.

I am the vine, ye are the branches: He
that abideth in me, and I in him, the
same bringeth forth much fruit: for
without me ye can do nothing.

—John 15:1-5

No man can succeed in life without the help of God.
Every effort will amount to nothing outside Him. It's

like trying to fill a basket with water! Just imagine the description our Lord gave when He said, He is the Vine and we are the branches.

Going by this description of our Lord, the continuous existence of the branch and it's bearing of fruit is dependent on the vine. The branch can only live because the vine is there for support. Only those people who are prepared to rely on God will make it to the end and excel. This is a divine principle and we must all get acquainted with it. This is the only path that leads to success and victorious living. Hear what the psalmist says:

> *Except the LORD build the house, they labour in vain that build it: except the LORD keep the city, the watchman waketh but in vain.*

> **—Psalm 127:1**

Let us move to the New Testament and consider what Paul the apostle said in relation to this:

> *So then it is not of him that willeth, nor of him that runneth, but of God that sheweth mercy.*

> **—Romans 9:16**

This book is written for any person who has a sincere desire for excellence. It contains the principles of soaring high like the eagles using Isaiah 40:31 as the background scripture:

But they that wait upon the LORD shall renew their strength; they shall mount up with wings as eagles; they shall run, and not be weary; and they shall walk, and not faint.

—Isaiah 40:31

Every blessing of God comes with condition. Only those that will wait on the Lord shall have their strength renewed to soar high like the eagles. This blessing will only become a mirage when the condition is not fulfilled. There is a price tag on every award. Once the condition is met the blessing shall be yours.

This book is an urgent call for all, no matter your sphere of life, to leverage on the greatness of God for excellence. And if you are that person who is so passionate about leaving your average position to move to the top, I would like to invite you to come on board with me in this journey.

STEPHEN IFEKOYA
Johannesburg, South Africa.

CHAPTER ONE

To whom then will ye liken God? or
what likeness will ye compare unto him?

Have ye not known? have ye not heard?
hath it not been told you from the
beginning? have ye not understood from
the foundations of the earth?

It is he that sitteth upon the circle of
the earth, and the inhabitants thereof
are as grasshoppers; that stretcheth out
the heavens as a curtain, and spreadeth
them out as a tent to dwell in:

That bringeth the princes to nothing; he
maketh the judges of the earth as vanity.

—Isaiah 40:18,21-23

THE GREATNESS OF GOD

The greatness of our God speaks of His reliability. It is
not wise to rely on somebody who is working under
another person's authority or control. A subordinate

is still looking unto the boss for help. Why then should one rely on such a person? Wisdom advises that we rely on the person who doesn't need another person's help. This is the case with the God we are serving. He is the greatest in heaven and on earth and everything revolves around Him: "**For by him were all things created, that are in heaven, and that are in earth, visible and invisible, whether they be thrones, or dominions, or principalities, or powers: all things were created by him, and for him: And he is before all things, and by him all things consist.**"—Colossians 1:16-17.

We cannot compare Him with anyone because He has no equal. He sits upon the circle of the earth and the inhabitants are like grasshoppers when compared with Him. This picture portrays Him as the one that is in control on earth. This scripture went further to say that He stretches out the heavens like curtains and spreads them out like a tent to dwell in and no one could question Him. This is because He controls all the heavens as well. It is only whatever He says that will come to pass because there are no two bosses in heaven and on earth when it comes to what should be done:

> *Who is he who speaks and it comes to pass, if the Lord has not authorized and commanded it?*

> **—Lamentations 3:37 [AMP]**

Listen, it is only whatever God authorizes that will happen. This means that all authority and power are under His control. And this was exercised by our Lord

Jesus Christ during His earthly ministry and was transferred to mankind:

> *Then he called his twelve disciples together, and gave them power and authority over all devils, and to cure diseases.*

—Luke 9:1

When Moses exercised this authority, the magicians of Pharaoh and the children of Israel confessed the greatness of God:

> *And the magicians did so with their enchantments to bring forth lice, but they could not: so there were lice upon man, and upon beast.*
>
> *Then the magicians said unto Pharaoh, This is the finger of God: and Pharaoh's heart was hardened, and he hearkened not unto them; as the LORD had said.*

—Exodus 8:18-19

The magicians of Pharaoh understood that day that it is God that is in control. Their power was limited but that of our God had no limit. They therefore had no other choice than to confess the greatness of the God we are serving. They were not afraid to tell their boss (Pharaoh) this truth even though he didn't agree with them.

Hear the confession of the children of Israel when they saw the greatness of God:

> *And the LORD said unto Moses, Stretch out thine hand over the sea, that the waters may come again upon the Egyptians, upon their chariots, and upon their horsemen.*
>
> *And Moses stretched forth his hand over the sea, and the sea returned to his strength when the morning appeared, and the Egyptians fled against it; and the LORD overthrew the Egyptians in the midst of the sea.*
>
> *And the waters returned, and covered the chariots, and the horsemen, and all the host of Pharaoh that came into the sea after them; there remained not so much as one of them.*
>
> *But the children of Israel walked upon dry land in the midst of the sea, and the waters were a wall unto them on their right hand, and on their left.*
>
> **Thus the LORD saved Israel that day out of the hand of the Egyptians; and Israel saw the Egyptians dead upon the sea shore.**
>
> **And Israel saw that great work which the LORD did upon the Egyptians: and the**

people feared the LORD, and believed the LORD, and his servant Moses.

—Exodus 14:26-31

It takes only a GREAT God to do a GREAT work. And it takes only a GREAT God to convince a GREAT people of His reliability.

Indeed, we are serving a great God whose greatness is incomparable with any other god. The kingdom of hell confessed His greatness through the magicians of Pharaoh when they saw a superior power as they have never seen before. Likewise, the kingdom of God confessed His greatness through the children of Israel after seeing such amazement as they have never seen before.

Moses who was used by God was not left out in the confession of the greatness of God. He was filled with awe of God after seeing what God had used him to do against the Egyptians. He went into a wild joy such that He became a powerful choir master. Listen to him and the children of Israel singing their triumphant song on that memorable day:

Then sang Moses and the children of Israel this song unto the LORD, and spake, saying, I will sing unto the LORD, for he hath triumphed gloriously: the horse and his rider hath he thrown into the sea.

The LORD is my strength and song, and he is become my salvation: he is my God, and

I will prepare him an habitation; my father's God, and I will exalt him.

The LORD is a man of war: the LORD is his name.

Pharaoh's chariots and his host hath he cast into the sea: his chosen captains also are drowned in the red sea.

The depths have covered them: they sank into the bottom as a stone.

Thy right hand, O LORD, is become glorious in power: thy right hand, O LORD, hath dashed in pieces the enemy.

And in the greatness of thine excellency thou hast overthrown them that rose up against thee: thou sentest forth thy wrath, which consumed them as stubble . . .

—Exodus 15:1-7

Shortly before Moses ended his ministry, he wrote another song to give testimony about the greatness of God. All through his ministry, he had seen the faithfulness of God. There was no better way for him to express his delight in God than to put it in the wordings of this song. Listen to him:

Give ear, O ye heavens, and I will speak; and hear, O earth, the words of my mouth.

My doctrine shall drop as the rain, my speech shall distil as the dew, as the small rain upon the tender herb, and as the showers upon the grass:

Because I will publish the name of the LORD: ascribe ye greatness unto our God.

He is the Rock, his work is perfect: for all his ways are judgment: a God of truth and without iniquity, just and right is he . . .

—Deuteronomy 32:1-4

The testimony of Moses is that our God is a great God and very reliable. And the God of the bible days is still the God of our days. He has not changed. He remains the same forever. He is still doing great wonders even in our days:

For I am the LORD, I change not; therefore ye sons of Jacob are not consumed.

—Malachi 3:6

Many generations after Moses heard of the greatness of God and therefore made a conclusion of His reliability:

We have heard with our ears, O God, our fathers have told us, what work thou didst in their days, in the times of old.

How thou didst drive out the heathen with thy hand, and plantedst them; how thou didst afflict the people, and cast them out.

For they got not the land in possession by their own sword, neither did their own arm save them: but thy right hand, and thine arm, and the light of thy countenance, because thou hadst a favour unto them.

Thou art my King, O God: command deliverances for Jacob.

Through thee will we push down our enemies: through thy name will we tread them under that rise up against us.

For I will not trust in my bow, neither shall my sword save me.

But thou hast saved us from our enemies, and has put them to shame that hated us.

In God we boast all day long, and praise thy name for ever.

—Psalm 44:1-8

At this juncture, I would like to conclude just as the psalmist made his conclusion that the greatness of the God we are serving is unsearchable:

> *I will extol thee, my God, O king; and I will bless thy name for ever and ever.*
>
> *Every day will I bless thee; and I will praise thy name for ever and ever.*
>
> *Great is the LORD, and greatly to be praised; and his greatness is unsearchable.*

—Psalm 145:1-3

I am a living proof of the greatness of God in the area of Divine Health. I have lived for close to 17 years now without any illness and I move around every day. Not even a reason to take a pain relieving pill. I used to be very sick since I was born until four years after I gave my life to Christ and I told sickness it will never be my portion again. I asked myself, what will make a difference between me and an unbeliever if we still queue together to seek doctors' attention? And God has been upholding His word in my mouth.

I have also seen God healed very deadly diseases through my ministry and one of them was a young man with HIV and AIDS. This same person was healed of a disease that was making him to sweat profusely at night when sleeping to the extent that he would have need to change his wet clothing about 7 times before day break even during winter. I have also seen countless number of people being delivered of demonic attacks through my ministry; and a number of marriages about to break were restored. Countless number of other unimaginable things God has done.

I therefore want to say that every living person must build trust in this our God because we are serving a great God whose reliability is unmatchable by any other god.

CHAPTER TWO

Has thou not known? hast thou not
heard, that the everlasting God, the
LORD, the Creator of the ends of
the earth, fainteth not, neither is
weary? there is no searching of his
understanding.

He giveth power to the faint; and to
them that have no might he increaseth
strength.

Even the youths shall faint and be weary,
and the young men shall utterly fall:

—Isaiah 40:28-31

EVEN THE YOUTHS SHALL FAINT AND BE WEARY

We have been able to prove that God is the greatest in
heaven and on earth. He takes control of everything in
heaven and on earth and nothing can happen outside His
notice. In this chapter, we shall expose the weakness of

man to present the reason why we should leverage on the strength of this great God.

GOD'S SUPREMACY OVER MAN

The God we are serving does not faint or grow weary. Weariness and fainting can only be traced to man because he is limited in strength. The supremacy of God over man is because of His superhuman strength. Therefore, man has "human strength" while God has "superhuman strength". But God can deposit His "superhuman strength" into a man to become a "superhuman being". That was the case with the children of Israel when they left slavery in Egypt and were on their way to the Promised Land. They were in the wilderness for forty years and they lacked nothing. This was necessary because God was committed to taking them to the Promised Land because of His covenant with their forefather, Abraham:

> *Even when they had made for themselves a molten calf and said, This is your god, who brought you out of Egypt, and had committed great and contemptible blasphemies,*

> *You in Your great mercy forsook them not in the wilderness; the pillar of the cloud departed not from them by day to lead them in the way, nor the pillar of fire by night to light the way they should go.*

You also gave Your good Spirit to instruct them, and withheld not Your manna from them, and gave water for their thirst.

Forty years You sustained them in the wilderness; they lacked nothing, their clothes did not wear out, and their feet did not swell.

—Nehemiah 9:18-21 [AMP]

It takes only a superhuman being to wear clothes for forty years and will not wear out! That is amazing! It was possible because God put His superhuman strength into them. Why? *"He giveth power to the faint; and to them that have no might he increaseth strength"*. This is the supremacy of God over man. This is what makes Him to be God. Through Him the believers can do incredible things that will shock the unbelievers.

When the Lord enabled me, some years ago, to build a three-bedroom flat as a full-time pastor with a meager salary I could not believe it myself. Why? *It was by the finger of God*.

Also, for more than four years as a missionary, my children never stayed at home one day because we couldn't pay school fees. As a matter of fact, at the fifth year, we concluded payment of school fees for two of them before the end of the second month of the new session. It was amazing. In addition, my wife was able to enroll for a doctorate degree programme at the same time. All these were accomplished with little or no salary. When we decided to do a run-down of all our expenses for the

13

four years, we were astounded to see the huge amount of money we had spent. We were shocked to the bones by what we calculated. One of the leaders of our ministry whom we told was forced to ask if I was secretly doing an extra work with a very big organization collecting a fat salary. Why? *"Hast thou not known? Hast thou not heard, that the everlasting God, the LORD, the Creator of the ends of the earth, fainteth not, neither is weary? there is no searching of his understanding"*.

Truly, your brain is too small to search out the doings of the Almighty God. He operates in the supernatural realm too high for the human mind to comprehend. The more you try to think about His doings the more you are confused. What explanation can you give to His miracle of parting the Red Sea and just immediately the children of Israel were walking on the dry land in between two pillars of water? It was enough miracles for them to have walked on a wet ground as long as they will still be able to cross the Red Sea. But the Almighty God dried up the water to make it easier for His children to walk through, especially the little ones. That is how much God cares for you and me. With His superhuman strength, He takes us to our Promised Land. He hasn't taken us this far to abandon us at the middle of the road. His plan is to take us to our destinations. Therefore, arise and faint not because the Almighty God is your God.

EVEN THE YOUTHS SHALL FAINT AND YOUNG MEN SHALL FALL

Youths or young men are symbols of physical strength:

> *The glory of young men is their strength: and the beauty of old men is the gray head.*
>
> **—Proverbs 20:29**

Sometime ago I was watching some young men who were in their twenties playing football in the middle of the night when the weather has cool down. Barely fifteen minutes after kick-off I saw them sweating profusely. Before the end of the first forty-five minutes they were already looking very tired and weary. On that day, I understood that:

> **Even the youths shall faint and be weary, and the young men shall utterly fall:**
>
> **—Isaiah 40:30**

No amount of physical strength can take a man through success in life without the help of God. It will only take a time before the strength of man will wear out no matter how strong is the man. Human strength is limited. Listen to Paul the apostle:

> **So then [God's gift] is not a question of human will and human effort, but of God's mercy. [It depends not on one's own willingness nor on his strenuous**

exertion as in running a race, but on God's having mercy on him.]

—Romans 9:16 [AMP]

Failure awaits any person who looks forward to accomplishing anything through human strength. The strength of man can never take him to his destination. This was the conclusion Hannah made after her victory over barrenness. She was testifying from what she had experienced. Listen to her testimonies:

And Hannah prayed, and said, My heart rejoiceth in the LORD, mine horn is exalted in the LORD: my mouth is enlarged over mine enemies; because I rejoice in thy salvation.

There is none holy as the LORD: for there is none beside thee: neither is there any rock like our God.

Talk no more so exceeding proudly; let not arrogancy come out your mouth: for the LORD is a God of knowledge, and by him actions are weighed.

The bows of the mighty men are broken, and they that stumbled are girded with strength.

He will keep the feet of his saints, and the wicked shall be silent in darkness; for by strength shall no man prevail.

—1Samuel 2:1-4, 9

I have never in life accomplished anything through my human strength. I ended up in frustration at every point that I have ever relied on my strength or the strength of any man. It is an exhibition of pride and arrogance when we rely on human strength. It will always end up as a fruitless effort.

I CANNOT DO IT BY MY STRENGTH

Success in life is a product of **'I cannot do it by my strength'**. This is true because God can only have relationship with the humble. He resists the proud but gives an unusual grace to whoever that comes to Him with a heart of humility:

But he giveth more grace. Wherefore he saith, GOD RESISTETH THE PROUD, BUT GIVETH GRACE UNTO THE HUMBLE.

—James 4:6

God takes up our challenges whenever we humble ourselves and let Him know that we cannot do it by our strength. Listen to this piece of advice from God on this truth:

Then he answered and spake unto me, saying, This is the word of the LORD unto Zerubbabel, saying, Not by might, nor by power, but by my spirit, saith the LORD of hosts.

Who art thou, O great mountain? before Zerubbabel thou shalt become a plain: and he shall bring forth the headstone thereof with shoutings, crying, Grace, grace unto it.

Moreover the word of the LORD came unto me, saying,

The hands of Zerubbabel have laid the foundation of this house; his hands shall also finish it; and thou shalt know that the LORD of hosts hath sent me unto you.

—Zechariah 4:6-9

Might and power are two different words God used to signify human strength in this story. For any man to succeed in life, he must learn not to rely on his human strength. Through this attitude we can pull down any mountain or challenge that stands against our success. Why? Because such attitude releases double grace for a man to be able to accomplish a task. This has been God's method of getting things done through His servants.

For more clarity, let us consider in detail two different servants of God: Moses and Gideon.

MOSES

Moses was a product of **'I cannot do it by my strength'**. When God was handing over to him his calling (assignment) he gave God these two reasons why he was not qualified to do the job:

Listen to his first reason:

> **And Moses said unto God, Who am I, that I should go unto Pharaoh, and that I should bring forth the children of Israel out Egypt?**
>
> **—Exodus 3:11**

Moses was referring to human strength that comes from human's qualification or societal status. Pharaoh was the king of Egypt, the world power in those days, while Moses was a mere "shepherd boy" to Jethro, an unknown priest of Midian.

Listen to his second reason:

> **And Moses said unto the LORD, O my Lord, I am not eloquent, neither heretofore, nor since thou hast spoken unto thy servant: but I am slow of speech, and of a slow tongue**
>
> **—Exodus 4:10**

This time around, Moses was referring to another human strength that comes from human's gifting called eloquence or ability to talk fluently.

Testimonies that followed Moses:

This same Moses that disqualified himself became a mighty vessel in God's hand. God deposited his superhuman strength unto him because he humbled himself. Listen to his testimonies shortly after his death:

> **So Moses the servant of the LORD died there in the land of Moab, according to the word of the LORD.**
>
> **And he buried him in a valley in the land of Moab, over against Bethpeor: but no man knoweth of his sepulcher unto this day.**
>
> **And Moses was an hundred and twenty years old when he died: his eye was not dim, nor his natural force abated.**
>
> **And the children of Israel wept for Moses in the plains of Moab thirty days: so the days of weeping and mourning for Moses were ended**
>
> **—Deuteronomy 34:5–8**

We can identify the following testimonies about Moses from this story:

- Moses lived a very healthy life. He died when he was one hundred and twenty years old, yet his eyes were not weak nor his strength gone.

  Consider the case of another man of God, Eli the priest:

  Now Eli was ninety and eight years old; and his eyes were dim, that he could not see.

  —1Samuel 4:15

- Moses was so celebrated by God that he was buried by God Himself instead of man.
- Moses was so celebrated by man that the whole Israel mourned him for thirty days. They must have closed their businesses for a whole month because of his exit.

In addition, the event that took place on the Mountain of Transfiguration in Matthew 17:1-9 was another eye-opener to the fact that Moses was a celebrity of God. This happened about three thousand four hundred and seventy (3,470) years after his death.

In the story, Jesus took three of His disciples to a mountain and behold, Moses and Elijah appeared talking with Him. Later, a bright light from heaven overshadowed them and was followed with a voice that acknowledged Jesus as His beloved Son.

Two things that made this event to be very important are:

(a) Firstly, it was the second time a voice from heaven came to declare Jesus as the Son of God.

(b) Secondly, Jesus warned His disciples not to disclose what happened to anyone until He would have gone back to heaven.

From these two observations, we can conclude that this event must have been conveyed to discuss heavenly matter. God must have chosen Moses and Elijah for this sacred event because they were His celebrities. Anyone that says "I cannot do it by my strength" ends up in this manner.

GIDEON

Gideon was also a product of **'I cannot do it by my strength'**. When God was handing over to him his calling (assignment) he also gave God two reasons why he was not qualified to do the assignment:

> **And the angel of the LORD appeared unto him, and said unto him, The LORD is with thee, thou mighty man of valour.**
>
> **And Gideon said unto him, Oh my Lord, if the LORD be with us, why then**

is all this befallen us? and where be all his miracles which our fathers told us of, saying, Did not the LORD bring us up from Egypt? but now the LORD hath forsaken us, and delivered us into the hands of the Midianites.

And the LORD looked upon him, and said, Go in this thy might, and thou shalt save Israel from the hand of the Midianites: have not I sent thee?

And he said unto him, Oh my Lord, wherewith shall I save Israel? behold, my family is poor in Manaseh, and I am the least in my father's house.

And the LORD said unto him, Surely I will be with thee, and thou shalt smite the Midianites as one man.

—Judges 6:12-16

Gideon's first reason:

From this story, his first reason was his family's "status" or "strength". He came from a poor family: ". . . **behold, my family is poor in Manasseh**". He was therefore telling God that his family has no societal status to qualify him for such a great assignment. Because of this, he didn't see himself qualified for the job and therefore confessed this to the Lord who is able to release His strength on him. But the word of God says:

> But God hath chosen the foolish things of the world to confound the wise; and God hath chosen the weak things of the world to confound the things which are mighty;

> And base things of the world, and things which are despised, hath God chosen, yea, and things which are not, to bring to nought things that are:

> That no flesh should glory in his presence.

> **—1 Corinthians 1:27-29**

Gideon's second reason:

Gideon's second reason was his human "status" or "strength". He was the least (youngest) in his family: **". . . and I am the least in my father's house"**. He therefore felt he shouldn't be the one to carry out this assignment. But the word of God says:

> **. . . Not by might, nor by power, but by my spirit, saith the LORD of hosts**

> **—Zechariah 4:6**

Testimonies that followed Gideon:

It was true that Gideon disqualified himself but consider his testimonies:

Then Zebah and Zalmunna said, Rise thou, and fall upon us: for as the man is, so is his strength. And Gideon arose, and slew Zebah and Zalmunna, and took away the ornaments that were on their camels' necks.

Then the men of Israel said unto Gideon, Rule thou over us, both thou, and thy son, and thy son's son also: for thou hast delivered us from the hand of Midian.

And Gideon said unto them, I will not rule over you, neither shall my son rule over you: the LORD shall rule over you.

Thus was Midian subdued before the children of Israel, so that they lifted up their heads no more. And the country was in quietness forty years in the days of Gideon.

And Gideon the son of Joash died in a good old age, and was buried in the sepulchre of Joash his father, in Ophrah of the Abiezrites.

—Judges 8:21-23,28,32

Gideon truly disqualified himself but became a mighty vessel in God's hand. Because of his humility, God deposited his superhuman strength unto him.

We can therefore make a conclusion that Moses and Gideon excelled because they started from a point of '**I cannot do it by my strength**'. Nothing can be accomplished by our strength because we don't have what it takes. Failure awaits a man who wants to do it by himself. This was what made our Lord to say:

> **. . . for without me ye can do nothing.**
>
> **—John 15:5**

God has no interest in a man who thinks he can do it on its own. He believes only in a man who is ready to leverage on His strength. When we confess our inability the Lord comes in to do it. That was why Paul wrote this in his letter to the church at Corinth:

> **And he said unto me, *My grace is sufficient for thee: for my strength is made perfect in weakness.* Most gladly therefore will I rather glory in my infirmities, that the power of Christ may rest upon me.**
>
> **Therefore I take pleasure in infirmities, in reproaches, in necessities, in persecutions, in distresses for Christ's sake: for when I am weak, then am I strong.**
>
> **—2 Corinthians 12:9-10**

We are strong only when we allow the Lord to come in to help us. For He promised to help us:

> **For I the LORD thy God will hold thy right hand, saying unto thee, Fear not; I will help thee.**
>
> **Fear not, thou worm Jacob, and ye men of Israel; I will help thee, saith the LORD, and thy redeemer, the Holy One of Israel.**
>
> **—Isaiah 41:13-14**

Worm in this context signifies somebody who is helpless because he doesn't have the strength. I'm sure you are aware that worm doesn't have backbone that signifies strength. God has a specialty in helping the helpless. He is a specialist in helping somebody who has no strength to get to his destination. And this is possible whenever we express our inabilities (weaknesses) to Him. This is the only way by which He can release His strength upon us. It is only by His strength we can get to our destinations. Nobody can stop Him whenever He has decided to do anything. Pharaoh could not stop Him from bringing Israel out of slavery when He stretched out His right hand:

> **For the LORD of hosts hath purposed, and who shall disannul it? and his hand is stretched out, and who shall turn it back?**
>
> **—Isaiah 14:27**

When the Lord has come to help you the confidence is that you will get to where you are going because nobody can stop Him. All you need to do is to rely on Him. Confess your inability and He will come in to help you.

CHAPTER THREE

But they that wait upon the LORD shall
renew their strength . . .

—Isaiah 40:31

BUT THEY THAT WAIT ON
THE LORD

We have been able to establish the truth that nothing can
be accomplished outside God. Our success in this life
is tied to no other person but God. He is greater than
the greatest of all men and greater than the greatest of
all the gods. We therefore need to move from this point
by looking at how we can leverage on Him to be able to
reach our goal in life.

In this chapter, we shall consider how we can effectively
wait on this great God to be able to leverage on His
superhuman strength and accomplish great height.

THE ACT OF WAITING ON THE LORD

To act means to do something or to perform an action. Waiting on the Lord is an act that must be performed and it goes beyond just having head knowledge. It is a knowledge that must be put into an action. I have come to realize that many Christians end up with the head knowledge of many things in Christianity and never being able to perform the necessary actions. This is the reason why many are confused in the church today.

I will try to explain what waiting on the Lord means from two definitions of the word "wait":

(a) **First meaning of Waiting on the Lord**

Wait means to remain inactive or to be in a state of rest until something expected happens.

From this definition, **waiting on the Lord is the ability to maintain a state of rest while expecting something from God**.

Rest in this sense means not troubled, unruffled, not moved, undisturbed, not agitated or calm. At the state of rest the heart of the person is at peace knowing for certain that the situation is under God's control.

Job was a good example of a Christian who waited on the Lord until his deliverance was accomplished.

Firstly, there was a great expectation in his heart that God will come to his rescue and therefore decided to wait on Him:

> **If a man dies, shall he live again? All the days of my warfare and service I will wait, till my change and release shall come.**
>
> **—Job 14:14 [AMP]**

Secondly, he was at rest because he knew that his God is alive and will come to his rescue:

> **For I know that my redeemer liveth, and that he shall stand at the latter day upon the earth:**
>
> **—Job 19:25**

To maintain a state of rest is very important when a Christian is waiting on God for a need. It is one of those conditions God needed to be able to meet our needs. When we are at rest we cease from our own struggle of getting things done and allow God to come in to do what He had accomplished for us from the foundation of the world:

> **For we which have believed do enter into rest, as he said, AS I HAVE SWORN IN MY WRATH, IF THEY SHALL ENTER INTO MY REST: although the works were finished from the foundation of the world.**

For he spake in a certain place of the seventh day on this wise, AND GOD DID REST THE SEVENTH DAY FROM ALL HIS WORKS.

For if Jesus had given them rest, then would he not afterward have spoken of another day.

There remaineth therefore a rest to the people of God.

For he that is entered into his rest, he also hath ceased from his own works, as God did from his.

Let us labour therefore to enter into that rest, least any man fall after the same example of unbelief.

—Hebrews 4:3-4, 8-11

From this scripture, anyone who will be at rest must know that God had finished everything concerning him from the foundation and won't have any need to be troubled. You are troubled because you are ignorant of this truth. What I normally tell people is that I can't be troubled by whatever that is happening around me because I am a **finished product** in God's hand. What I do every day is to push through prayer while watching unto what God has for me. That is why the scripture encourages us to labour to enter into that rest God had accomplished for us. And this will take faith. Why?

Because you don't really know what God has for you tomorrow but you are just trusting Him and following him by faith. This is why the bible says in 2 Corinthians 5:7 that: "**for we walk by faith, not by sight**".

Faith is defined by the bible as:

> **Now faith is the substance of things hoped for, the evidence of things not seen.**
>
> **—Hebrews 11:1**

Faith is therefore based on what God says and not on our human feelings. It is the conviction of the reality of things we do not see; perceiving as a real fact what is not revealed to the human senses. Truly, faith has nothing to do with our five senses—vision, taste, hearing, smell and touch. It operates in the realm of the invisible concerning those things we hope for. Job would have died if he was moved by what he was seeing around him—lost all his children, lost all his wealth, the wife abandoned him because he refused to renounce his God and was afflicted with sores all over his body.

You are troubled because you don't have faith in the God you are serving. Faith gives us rest from all troubles. God didn't promise us a trouble-free life. What He promised is that trouble will not destroy us because He will be with us in time of trouble. God didn't promise Daniel that he won't be thrown into the den of lions. What God promised him was that the mouths of the lions will be closed. Likewise, God didn't promise Shadrach, Meshach and Abednego that they won't be thrown into the fire.

What God promised them was that fire won't burn them because He will be in the fire with them.

When we know all these things, our faith in the God we are serving will be strong enough to give us rest (peace of mind) as we wait on Him.

(b) **Second meaning of Waiting on the Lord**

Wait is also defined as hoping or expecting that something will happen.

From this definition, waiting on the Lord is the ability to build hope or expectation in God because of His reliability.

Consider what the psalmist said:

> **Deliver me, O my God, out of the hand of the wicked, out of the hand of the unrighteous and cruel man.**
>
> **For thou art my hope, O Lord GOD: thou art my trust from my youth.**
>
> **—Psalm 71:4-5**

Hope rises in a man's heart as a result of trust or confidence. You can only put hope in someone who has earned your trust. David trusted God so much that hope rises up in his heart whenever a challenge comes up. This was why the size of Goliath could not stop him. When others were seeing Goliath as a giant he was seeing him as a small boy who has no respect for the God of the Israelites. All he saw was a small boy trying to give him a fight. Not even Saul was enough to stop him. All David needed to do so that Saul could release him to fight Goliath was to share testimonies of his exploits:

> **And David said to Saul, Let no man's heart fail because of him; thy servant will go and fight with this Philistine.**

> **And Saul said to David, Thou art not able to go against this Philistine to fight with him: for thou art but a youth, and he a man of war from his youth.**

> **And David said unto Saul, Thy servant kept his father's sheep, and there came a lion, and a bear, and took a lamb out of the flock:**

> **And I went out after him, and smote him, and delivered it out of his mouth: and when he arose against me, I caught him by his beard, and smote him, and slew him.**

> **Thy servant slew both the lion and the bear: and this uncircumcised Philistine shall be as one of them, seeing he hath defiled the armies of the living God.**

> **David said moreover, The LORD that delivered me out of the paw of the**

> lion, and out of the paw of the bear, he will deliver me out of the hand of this Philistine. And Saul said unto David, Go, and the LORD be with thee.

> **—1 Samuel 17:32-37**

Hope is the confident expectation, the sure certainty that what God has promised in His word is true. David was very confident that he will defeat Goliath because he trusted God and this gave rise to hope in his heart. He was so sure that the God that gave him victory over those deadly animals will surely show up. More so, Goliath was defiling the Name of the God of Israel.

As we wait on God hoping in His faithfulness and reliability, He will show Himself strong on our behalf.

PRINCIPLES OF WAITING ON THE LORD

There are virtues we must possess to make our waiting on the Lord to be effective. Our God is not a magician but a Miracle Worker. He is a faithful God and not a deceiver. He is a God of principles. He meets the needs of those that follow His principles when they wait on Him. Let us therefore consider these eight principles of how we can wait on the Lord and achieve our goals:

PRINCIPLE OF PATIENCE:

Effective waiting on the Lord takes patience.

Patience is the ability to accept or tolerate delay, trouble or suffering without getting angry; it is the state of endurance under difficult circumstances; persevering in the face of delay. It is a virtue needed by every person who wants to wait on God and achieve the expected goal.

I want to say that patience is a very critical need in the church today. We are in a generation of "I want it quickly" and not being mindful of God's timing. God is too slow for many Christians today. The major setback the church has suffered today is as a result of impatience. It was the impatience of Sarah that made Hagar to come into the life of Abraham and this brought confusion twice that nearly affected Abraham's home:

> **Now Sarai Abram's wife bare him no children: and she had an handmaid, an Egyptian, whose name was Hagar.**
>
> **And Sarai said unto Abram, Behold now, the LORD hath restrained me from bearing: I pray thee, go in unto my maid; it may be that I may obtain children by her. And Abram hearkened to the voice of Sarai.**
>
> **And Sarai Abram's wife took Hagar her maid the Egyptian, after Abram had dwelt ten years in the land of Canaan, and gave her to her husband Abram to be his wife.**

And he went in unto Hagar, and she conceived: and when she saw that she had conceived, her mistress was despised in her eyes.

And Sarai said unto Abram, My wrong be upon thee: I have given my maid into thy bosom; and when she saw that she had conceived, I was despised in her eyes: the LORD judge between me and thee.

But Abram said unto Sarai, Behold, thy maid is in thy hand; do to her as it pleaseth thee. And when Sarai dealt hardly with her, she fled from her face.

—Genesis 16:1-6

The quick repentance of Sarah and Abraham's sensitivity delivered them from separation. It happened again after Hagar had her child, Ishmael:

And Sarah saw the son of Hagar the Egyptian, which she had born unto Abraham, mocking.

Wherefore she said unto Abraham, Cast out this bondwoman and her son: for the son of this bondwoman shall not be heir with my son, even with Isaac.

And the thing was very grievous in Abraham's sight because of his son.

And God said unto Abraham, Let it not be grievous in thy sight because of the lad, and because of thy bondwoman; in all that Sarah hath said unto thee, hearken unto her voice; for in Isaac shall thy seed be called.

—Genesis 21:9-12

This time around, it was through Hagar's son that the enemy attacked. Enemy's plan was overthrown because Sarah understood the Divine purpose of God concerning Isaac as the heir to Abraham. This made God to intervene quickly so that His eternal purpose could stand.

Patience is needed to bring the church into alignment with God's plan and purpose. God directs things according to His plan and not according to any man's plan. Isaac came at the set time of God and not according to Abraham's plan or Sarah's plan:

And the LORD visited Sarah as he had said, and the LORD did unto Sarah as he had spoken.

For Sarah conceived, and bare Abraham a son in his old age, at the set time of which God had spoken to him.

—Genesis 21:1-2

There is a set time for every purpose under the sun.

When the Lord spoke to me about my mission assignment I thought it was going to be immediately. I took time to patiently wait on the Lord. At a point I thought it wouldn't happen again. But on the seventh year and ninth month, an unusual door was opened that all I needed to bring the assignment to pass was handed over to me. It took waiting on the Lord patiently to bring it to pass. We run into problems when we want to run ahead of God. All the pain Abraham and Sarah went through would have been averted through patience. They entered into trouble because Sarah was trying to fix things by herself. A little more patience would have averted all the trouble they passed through. God is never too slow to meet our needs. It takes patience to wait on Him to bring to pass His promises:

> **Cast not away therefore your confidence, which hath great recompence of reward.**
>
> **For ye have need of patience, that, after ye have done the will of God, ye might receive the promise.**
>
> **FOR YET A LITTLE WHILE, AND HE THAT SHALL COME WILL COME, AND WILL NOT TARRY.**
>
> **—Hebrews 10:35-37**

The School of Patience is a necessary school for any person who desires to receive the promise of God.

When a man is not properly informed the outcome will always be a deformation of destiny. This generation needs proper information about the importance of patience. Fulfillment of destiny becomes a mirage when a man is unequipped with patience. Many visions have died because of impatience. Gehazi ended up with leprosy because of lack of patience. He wanted to run faster than Elisha his master and therefore ended his destiny in a ghastly accident. I don't think it was God's will for him to end the way he ended.

Anyone that wants to fulfill destiny must learn to patiently wait on God. Our Master Jesus is a good example of those that patiently waited on God to fulfill destiny. He was patiently following the Father and never moved ahead of Him:

> **Then said Jesus unto them, When ye have lifted up the Son of man, then shall ye know that I am he, and that I do nothing of myself; but as my Father hath taught me, I speak these things**
>
> **—John 8:28**

Effective waiting on the Lord demands patience. When we patiently wait on God, He will hear our cry:

> **I waited patiently for the LORD; and he inclined unto me, and heard my cry.**
>
> **—Psalm 40:1**

We must patiently cry unto Him until he hears us.

PRINCIPLE OF PRAYER:

Effective waiting on the Lord takes prayer.

Prayer is the only way to carry our burden to the Lord. God moves mountain but prayer moves God. If our prayer is the only thing that can move God into action then we must pray. A prayerful Christian moves mountain while a prayer less Christian tolerates the mountain. Prayer is not a choice but a must. You have not started praying because you are satisfied with your challenge:

A prayerful Christian takes control and dictates for others to follow:

> **. . . The effectual fervent prayer of a righteous man availeth much.**
>
> **Elias was a man subject to like passions as we are, and he prayed earnestly that it might not rain: and it rained not on the earth by the space of three years and six months.**
>
> **And he prayed again, and the heaven gave rain, and the earth brought forth her fruit.**
>
> **—James 5:16-18**

Prayer is a virtue every living person needs to move to the next level. That was the case with Hannah to be able to move from being a barren woman to becoming a mother. She was able to move God into action through her prayer. She had been going for the yearly sacrifice as a barren woman until that particular year when she realized her status must change. That was possible at the altar of prayer. Nothing moves until it is pushed. Her prayer pushed her into her destiny of birthing the long awaited prophet in Israel called Samuel. She decided to wait on the Lord in prayer until her case received attention by the God of heaven. She was so tired of her situation that she lost her appetite. She was no longer interested in any other thing but to have her son. She waited on God in prayer until she was taken to be a drunkard. She prayed until her countenance changed:

> **And it came to pass, as she continued praying before the LORD, that Eli marked her mouth.**

> **Now Hannah, she spake in her heart; only her lips moved, but her voice was not heard: therefore Eli thought she had been drunken.**

> **And Eli said unto her, How long wilt thou be drunken? Put away thy wine from thee.**

> **And Hannah answered and said, No, my lord, I am a woman of a sorrowful spirit: I have drunk neither wine nor**

> strong drink, but have poured out my soul before the LORD.
>
> Count not thine handmaid for a daughter of Belial: for out of the abundance of my complaint and grief have I spoken hitherto.
>
> Then Eli answered and said, Go in peace: and the God of Israel grant thee thy petition that thou hast asked of him
>
> And she said, let thine handmaid find grace in thy sight. So the woman went her way, and did eat, and her countenance was no more sad.
>
> **—1 Samuel 1:12-18**

Waiting on the Lord in prayer is to pray until something happens. Imagine the prayer that made a woman to be counted to be a drunkard. That is the prayer that brings uncommon testimonies; a prayer that God will not be able to resist. Listen to her testimony:

> Wherefore it came to pass, when the time was come about after Hannah had conceived, that she bare a son, and called his name Samuel, saying, because I have asked him of the LORD.
>
> And when she had weaned him, she took him up with her, with three bullocks, and

one ephah of flour, and a bottle of wine, and brought him unto the house of the LORD in Shilloh: and the child was young.

And they slew a bullock, and brought the child to Eli.

And she said, O my lord, as thy soul liveth, my lord, I am the woman that stood by thee here, praying unto the LORD.

For this child I prayed; and the LORD hath given me my petition which I asked of him.

—1 Samuel 1:20,24-27

Testimonies are around the corner whenever a man decides to wait on the Lord in prayer.

I remember a sister in one of the churches I was the pastor several years ago. She had three big fibroids that never allowed her pregnancy to stay. She was given money to go for an operation but she refused to do that. Instead, she decided to sow the money into my wife's school. One day, I was ministering during one of our first day of the month prayer and she was in attendance. The Lord opened my eyes and I saw the Lord operating the womb of a sister. I made a prophetic utterance to seal what the Lord was doing. All I could remember was that I noticed that this sister was praying as Hannah prayed and tears were rolling down her eyes. When she got home after the service, she went to the toilet. To her amazement, two of those fibroids came out. Today, she is a mother. All was accomplished at the altar of waiting on the Lord in prayer.

I don't know, maybe your testimonies are being delayed because you have been delaying your waiting on God in prayer. Take a decision today and you will be the next person to share testimonies.

PRINCIPLE OF FASTING:

Effective waiting on the Lord takes fasting.

Fasting is a step to crucify the flesh so that it can be under the control of the spirit man. It is an exercise to afflict the soul of a man so that the spirit can be lifted; to lift the bondage of wickedness; to undo the heavy burdens in the heart; to let the oppressed receive freedom; and to break every yoke tormenting the man:

> **Behold, ye fast for strife and debate, and to smite with the fist of wickedness: ye shall not fast as ye do this day, to make your voice to be heard on high.**

> **Is it such a fast that I have chosen? a day for a man to afflict his soul? is it to bow down his head as a bulrush, and to spread sackcloth and ashes under him? Wilt thou call this a fast, and an acceptable day to the LORD?**

> Is not this the fast that I have chosen? To loose the bands of wickedness, to undo the heavy burdens, and to let the oppressed go free, and that ye break every yoke?

> —Isaiah 58:4-6

The voice of a Christian will be lifted so high when waiting on the Lord through fasting. It is a principle of God to uplift His servants. Moses did it for forty days and forty nights and his life never remained the same:

> And the LORD said unto Moses, Write thou these words: for after the tenor of these words I have made a covenant with thee and with Israel.

> And he was there with the LORD forty days and forty nights; he did neither eat bread, nor drink water. And he wrote upon the tables the words of the covenant, the ten commandments.

> And it came to pass, when Moses came down from mount Sinai with the two tables of testimony in Moses' hand, when he came down from the mount, that Moses wist not that the skin of his face shone while he talked with him.

> And when Aaron and all the children of Israel saw Moses, behold, the skin of

his face shone; and they were afraid to come nigh him.

—Exodus 34:27-30

The principle of Fasting while waiting on the Lord subdues the flesh so that the spirit man can be lifted to the presence of God for impartation. It takes a man to a realm where he will begin to stand tall among others.

Fasting is for those who desire to become spiritual giants. A man who is only giving to eating always and fast less will only remain as a spiritual dwarf. Fasting builds up the spiritual muscle needed for the spiritual battle we are facing every day. A man that hardly fast will face spiritual embarrassment. Jesus taught His disciples this principle when they were humiliated by a demon:

And when they were come to the multitude, there came to him a certain man, kneeling down to him and saying,

Lord, have mercy on my son: for he is lunatic, and sore vexed: for ofttimes he falleth into the fire, and oft into the water.

And I brought him to thy disciples, and they could not cure him.

Then Jesus answered and said, O faithless and perverse generation, how long shall

I be with you? how long shall I suffer you? Bring him hither to me.

And Jesus rebuked the devil; and he departed out of him: and the child was cured from that very hour.

Then came the disciples to Jesus apart, and said, Why could not we cast him out?

And Jesus said unto them, Because of your unbelief: for verily I say unto you, If ye have faith as a grain of mustard seed, ye shall say unto this mountain, Remove hence to yonder place; and it shall remove; and nothing shall be impossible unto you.

Howbeit this kind goeth not out but by prayer and fasting.

—Matthew 17:14-21

Jesus was only making His disciples to realize that there are some grounds you cannot break until you support your prayer with fasting. If you must allow God to take you to higher grounds then you must wait on Him with fasting.

In our ministry, the Lord told us to begin to join the Jews in celebrating Esther fast every year. This demands our fasting for three days without food and water. The very year we started, the Lord reversed the irreversible decree written against my mission work. It was amazing! This book you are reading is one of the many testimonies that followed the last Esther fast we had. It took barely two weeks for this book to be written, typed and sent for publishing. Ponder over these testimonies yourself and take a decision if you will join the chariot or not. I am not of them that draw back on this matter. Waiting on the Lord will be very effective when we do it with fasting. It is a principle of God and He has given us enough testimonies to authenticate it.

PRINCIPLE OF THE WORD OF GOD:

Effective waiting on the Lord takes studying and acting the Word of God.

The Word of God is God Himself. You cannot separate Him from His Word just as you cannot separate a man from his word. That is why I can say "he has given me his word". The meaning is that he has given his consent because he has spoken.

The Word of God can do whatever God can do. Hear it from the centurion whose servant was healed:

> **And when Jesus was entered into Capernaum, there came unto him a centurion, beseeching him,**
>
> **And saying, Lord, my servant lieth at home sick of the palsy, grievously tormented.**

And Jesus saith unto him, I will come and heal him.

The centurion answered and said, Lord, I am not worthy that thou shouldest come under my roof: but speak the word only, and my servant shall be healed.

For I am a man under authority, having soldiers under me: and I say to this man, Go, and he goeth; and to another, Come, and he cometh; and to my servant, Do this, and he doeth it.

And Jesus said unto the centurion, Go thy way; and as thou hast believe, so be it done unto thee. And his servant was healed in the selfsame hour.

—Matthew 8:5-9, 13

My wife had serious bleeding for seven days when our first child was fifty-eight days old in the womb. After the bleeding the doctor advised that she should go for a scan test so that they could ascertain the state of the baby. She came back home with the result that they are not sure if the baby is still living because of the adverse effect of the bleeding. They said there was no evidence to show that the baby is still living. Since I knew my bible very well, I just retorted that she had only come home with the doctor's report and not the Lord's report. I told her that the baby in the womb can hear the word of God whether living or dead. I knew that Lazarus heard the word of God as a dead man after four days in the grave. And I spoke the word of God to the baby that God has not given me a baby that will die but a living baby. Two weeks later she went for another scan test and came back with a new report that the baby is doing well. Though I couldn't touch the baby to lay my hands on her but she could hear the word of God that has no barrier. That baby that scan test declared dead in the womb will be fifteen years next month and will enter university in less than two years' time.

There is nothing impossible for the word of God since nothing shall be impossible with God. His Word is creative. He created all things by His Word and sustains them with the power in His Word:

> **For the word of God is quick, and powerful, and sharper than any twoedged sword, piercing even to the dividing asunder of soul and spirit, and of the joints and marrow, and is a discerner of the thoughts and intents of the heart.**
>
> **—Hebrews 4:12**

> **Who being the brightness of his glory, and the express image of his person, and upholding all things by the word of his power . . .**
>
> **—Hebrews 1:3**

A Christian is as powerful as the amount of the word of God that resides in him. A wordless Christian is a powerless Christian. Even our Lord Jesus conquered Satan with the written word of God. It is the need of the hour. Christians must start studying the word of God and stop gallivanting around with empty words. We are under pressure because we like pleasure. We celebrate emptiness a lot in the church. When a Christian is filled to the brim with the word of God he will explode. The church must grow from a wordless church to a word-base church where signs and wonders will be our daily bread.

PRINCIPLE OF SILENCE BEFORE GOD:

Effective waiting on the Lord demands that we maintain silence.

When waiting on the Lord, a Christian is supposed to be still so that he can ward off every noise that have overcrowded his heart. Waiting on the Lord is an attempt to seek for direction in a time of need. It is not possible for a man to hear the voice of God when the heart is noisy. That is why God said we should be still:

> **He maketh wars to cease unto the end of the earth; he breaketh the bow, and cutteth the spear in sunder; he burneth the chariot in the fire.**
>
> **Be still, and know that I am God: I will be exalted among the heathen, I will be exalted in the earth.**
>
> **—Psalm 46:9-10**

Those challenges we experience are the wars the bible is talking about in this scripture. There are noises everywhere during a war. The only way you can clearly hear the voice of God for direction at such a time is to shut the door of your heart against such wars. When you have done that, God can then speak to direct you safely. Let us learn from David:

> And it came to pass, when David and his men were come to Ziklag on the third day, that the Amalekites had invaded the south, and Ziklag, and smitten Ziklag, and burned it with fire;

> And had taken the women captives, that were therein: they slew not any, either great or small, but carried them away, and went on their way.

> So David and his men came to the city, and, behold, it was burned with fire; and their wives, and their sons, and their daughters, were taken captives.

> Then David and the people that were with him lifted up their voice and wept, until they had no more power to weep.

> And David's two wives were taken captives, Ahinoam the Jezreelitess and Abigail the wife of Nabal the Carmelite.

And David was greatly distressed; for the people spake of stoning him, because the soul of all the people was grieved, every man for his sons and for his daughters: but David encouraged himself in the LORD his God.

And David said to Abiathar the priest, Ahimelech's son, I pray thee, bring me hither the ephod. And Abiathar brought thither the ephod to David.

And David enquired at the LORD, saying, Shall I pursue after this troop? shall I overtake them? And he answered him, Pursue: for thou shalt surely overtake them, and without fail recover all.

—1 Samuel 30:1-8

At the end, David recovered all as the Lord has spoken. But the principle is that, though David was distressed as well but he shut the door of his heart against the sorrow to be able to wait on the Lord for direction. The Lord directed him appropriately and he followed His leading. At the time you are fainting, just retreat to the Lord shutting your heart against your situation. As you do that, you will receive the right direction from the Lord and come out of your confusion with a new strength.

I needed about US $3,012 when I was to process my family's residence permit on our mission field. We were given one month to start the processing else they must leave the country. I have never faced such a difficult time since I became an adult. I approached two people for help but both proved abortive. It was one other friend that I approached that gave me about US $300 after being humiliated and I had to ask God for forgiveness. Close to one month we have only gotten about US $964. My heart was overwhelmed with sorrow because I was imagining where the balance will come from. One morning, as I was getting up to call my family for our morning prayer, the Lord said I should lay an "altar of Ebenezer" as Samuel did when Israel was being tormented by the Philistine. I told my family and we obeyed the instruction. I would like to tell you that the Lord provided all the money needed at the right time without borrowing from any human being. My heart was overwhelmed but I decided to shut my heart against the sorrow so that I could seek God's face for direction. That was why I could hear the instruction from Him that morning. I cannot explain till tomorrow how the Lord provided the money. It has been one of the most amazing miracles I have seen in my life as a Christian. We need to learn to be still before Him in the midst of our trouble whenever we wait on Him for our need.

PRINCIPLE OF HARD WORK:

Waiting on the Lord can only be very effective through hard work.

I want to say that hard work will make a man to excel in life. Whatever your goal is, you can get there once you are willing to work hard. Laziness is not of God and it should not be tolerated. Any organization that is filled with lazy men and women will never excel like others. It's a matter of time; such organization will hit the rock and close up. All the men and women that have ever walked with God and excelled made it through hard work.

I would like to draw your attention to Paul who excelled above all the apostles he met in the faith. His letters to the churches and individuals are evidences of his hard work. Listen to his comment when he was exposing the secret of his success:

> **For I am the least [worthy] of the apostles, who am not fit or deserving to be called an apostle, because I once wronged and pursued and molested the church of God [oppressing it with cruelty and violence].**
>
> **But by the grace (the unmerited favor and blessing) of God I am what I am, and His grace toward me was not [found to be] for nothing (fruitless and without effect). In fact, I worked harder than all of them [the apostles], though it was not really I, but the grace (the unmerited favor and blessing) of God which was with me.**
>
> **—1 Corinthians 15:9-10 [AMP]**

Paul, unlike many Christians, was not hiding under the grace of God; but worked harder than all the other apostles whom he met in faith.

As we wait on God with our hard work, nothing stops us from soaring high like the eagles.

PRINCIPLE OF ACCEPTING CHALLENGES:

As we wait on the Lord, we should be ready to accept whatever challenge the Lord brings our way.

Many people don't like accepting challenges and thereby walk away from their blessings. I would like to affirm that challenges are opportunities to our success turned upside down. To the physical eyes, it might resemble a problem but to the spiritual eyes, it is an opportunity that leads to success.

Challenges can only end up refining our lives and never to destroy us:

> **Behold, I have refined thee, but not with silver; I have chosen thee in the furnace of affliction.**
>
> **—Isaiah 48:10**

When we confront our challenges with great determination it will only lead us into our much awaited success and promotion.

A very good example was when young David was sent by his father to go and give food to his brothers at the war front and he met the Philistine Giant called Goliath harassing the army of Israel to come up with one soldier to face him in a battle. Saul was there but not willing to accept the challenge despite his stature as described:

> **Kish had a son named Saul, a choice young man and handsome; among all the Israelites there was not a man more handsome than he. He was a head taller than any of the people.**

> **—1 Samuel 9:2 [AMP]**

Despite this stature of Saul, Goliath came with his challenge but he couldn't accept the challenge. But a very young man that Goliath could not even notice on time because of his small size accepted the challenge of removing this shame from the people of God:

> **And there went out a champion out of the camp of the Philistines, named Goliath, of Gath, whose height was six cubits and a span.**

> **And he stood and cried unto the armies of Israel, and said unto them, Why are ye come out to set your battle in array? am not I a Philistine, and ye servants to Saul? choose you a man for you, and let him come down to me.**

> If he be able to fight with me, and to kill me, then will we be your servants: but if I prevail against him, and kill him, then shall ye be our servants, and serve us.
>
> And the Philistine said, I defy the armies of Israel this day, give me a man, that we may fight together.
>
> When Saul and all Israel heard those words of the Philistine, they were dismayed, and greatly afraid.
>
> And the Philistine drew near morning and evening, and presented himself forty days.
>
> —1 Samuel 17:4,8-11,16

For forty days Saul and other soldiers could not take up the challenge until the young David came to confront Goliath and destroyed him:

> So David prevailed over the Philistine with a sling and with a stone, and smote the Philistine, and slew him; but there was no sword in the hand of David.
>
> —1 Samuel 17:50

David didn't know that the challenge was an opportunity God brought his way for his promotion. He got his promotion after the victory because not even Saul could stop him. Without any interview for a job, David was promoted from following his father's sheep to become the head of the army of Israel. All because he accepted the challenge:

> **And David went out whithersoever Saul sent him, and behaved himself wisely: and Saul set him over the men of war, and he was accepted in the sight of all the people, and also in the sight of Saul's servants.**
>
> **—1 Samuel 18:5**

The greater our challenge the greater our promotion. David had such a great promotion because he risked his life. Listen to how Jonathan explained it to his father Saul:

> **And Jonathan spake good of David unto Saul his father, and said unto him, Let not the king sin against his servant, against David, because he hath not sinned against thee, and because his works have been to thee-ward very good:**
>
> **For he did put his life in his hand, and slew the Philistine, and the Lord wrought a great salvation for all Israel: thou sawest it, and didst rejoice . . .**
>
> **—1 Samuel 19:4-5**

Accepting challenges is an opportunity for our promotion. We turn away our opportunity when we shy away from accepting a challenge.

There came a time that our ministry needed an accountant and there was none available. My boss, the State Overseer called me and said I will have to take up the job. It was a big challenge because I am an Industrial Mathematician and not an Accountant. I accepted the challenge and did very well on the job that lasted for two years. What helped me was the knowledge I acquired in an elective course (Principles of Accounting) I offered in my third year at the university. I took up the challenge when the Lord quickened me to offer this course because it wasn't a common thing to see a pure science student offering such a course from the Faculty of Business Management. The Lord who sees ahead of time understood that in about 17 years after I would have need of using the knowledge to be acquired to help my ministry. I willingly accepted the challenge of taking up the job and ended up with these testimonies: the normal story of owing staff salaries became a thing of the past; there was enough money in the account of the ministry as I was leaving; and the National headquarters of the ministry was collecting the weekly remittances regularly. That was an Industrial Mathematician who took up the challenge of the job of an Accountant. It was this job that the Lord used to quicken my mission call that had tarried for more than seven years.

As you wait on God and accepting whatever challenge He brings your way, you are definitely on your way to the top. It is a trial or mountain you must climb to take you to your next level:

PRINCIPLE OF FOCUS:

Maintaining focus is very important when waiting on God.

Maintaining focus is to concentrate attention or energy on something. When a man maintains focus he will surely get to his destination but any man that is easily distracted will end up along the way. It takes determination to maintain focus.

Our Lord excelled in His ministry because He was very focus. He understood why he was on earth and therefore maintained His focus. And when it was time to accomplish His purpose He made the necessary preparations and never allowed Himself to be distracted:

> **And it came to pass, when the time was come that he should be received up, he stedfastly set his face to go to Jerusalem,**
>
> **And sent messengers before his face: and they went, and entered into a village of the Samaritans, to make ready for him.**
>
> **—Luke 9:51-52**

Paul the apostle maintained his focus and determined not to be distracted not even by the afflictions that were waiting for him in Jerusalem where he was to end his ministry:

And now, you see, I am going to Jerusalem, bound by the [Holy] Spirit and obligated and compelled by the [convictions of my own] spirit, not knowing what will befall me there—

Except that the Holy Spirit clearly and emphatically affirms to me in city after city that imprisonment and suffering await me.

But none of these things move me; neither do I esteem my life dear to myself, if only I may finish my course with joy and the ministry which I have obtained from [which was entrusted to me by] the Lord Jesus, faithfully to attest to the good news (Gospel of God's grace (His unmerited favor, spiritual blessing, and mercy).

—Acts 20:22-24 [AMP]

Maintaining focus releases an unusual power for a man to keep going despite the challenges. Waiting on the Lord therefore becomes effective when we keep our focus.

BUT THEY THAT WAIT ON THE LORD

One of the rewards that follow those that wait on the Lord is that their strength shall be renewed. Waiting time is not wasting time. It is a time well spent for our strength to be renewed when we follow the principles of waiting on the Lord:

> **But they that wait upon the LORD shall renew their strength . . .**
>
> **—Isaiah 40:31**

Strength is what you need to be able to face the battle of this life. Your strength determines how strong you are. That is, you are as strong as your strength.

To renew is to make something new again or to restore it to its original condition. To renew strength therefore means restoration of strength. When we have gone through the battle of this life it will come to a time when we must go back to the Lord for renewal of our strength. At such a time, it will be too dangerous to continue the battle with the little strength that is left with us. This was the secret behind the success of our Lord. You will notice that so many times He withdrew even from His disciples to be alone with the Father. At the end, He was always coming out with His strength renewed:

> **But so much the more went there a fame abroad of him: and great multitudes came together to hear, and to be healed by him of their infirmities.**
>
> **And he withdrew himself into the wilderness, and prayed.**

> **And it came to pass on a certain day,**
> **as he was teaching, that there were**
> **Pharisees and doctors of the law sitting**
> **by, which were come out of every town**
> **of Galilee, and Judaea, and Jerusalem:**
> **and the power of the Lord was present**
> **to heal them.**

> —Luke5:15-17

Even Jesus needed to go and wait on the Lord. He was not distracted by the crowd that wanted to see Him. Many would have jumped out to the occasion raising their shoulders high because of the crowd waiting to see them. Look at the result, power of God was present just when He was still teaching the word. His strength was definitely renewed.

The ultimate was when He needed to face the inevitable death; He retrieved to go and wait on the Father in prayer taking His disciples along for support:

> **And he was withdrawn from them about**
> **a stone's cast, and kneeled down, and**
> **prayed,**

> **Saying, Father, if thou be willing,**
> **remove this cup from me: nevertheless**
> **not my will, but thine, be done.**

> **And there appeared an angel unto him**
> **from heaven, strengthening him.**

> **—Luke 22:41-43**

It was not easy for our Lord to die for us. Gospel of Mark explained it this way "**And saith unto them, My soul is exceeding sorrowful unto death: tarry ye here, and watch**"—Mark 14:34. Of course, our Lord was a man in the flesh and His strength was failing Him at this point in time. So, he needed to go and wait on the Lord for a new strength. At the end, His strength was renewed to be able to face the death that brought about the salvation of mankind.

Let us therefore learn from our Master so that when we wait on the Lord, we renew our strength for a new height.

Chapter Four

... they shall mount up with wings as
eagles; they shall run, and not be weary;
and they shall walk, and not faint.

—Isaiah 40:31

SOARING HIGH LIKE EAGLES

The first result that follows the people that wait on the
Lord is that they shall renew their strength and we have
discussed this in the previous chapter. In this chapter, we
shall discuss the remaining results that follow the people
that wait on the Lord; they are the following as stated in
the scripture above:

(a) They shall mount up with wings as eagles.

(b) They shall run, and not be weary.

(c) They shall walk, and not faint.

THEY SHALL MOUNT UP WITH WINGS AS EAGLES

Mounting up with wings as eagles means soaring high like the eagles. The first thing that must be noted is that the eagle is a special bird because of some remarkable features it possesses. Because of these features, the bible carefully uses this bird to explain what shall be the outcome of the Christians that wait on the Lord.

We shall therefore consider some of the features of the eagle bird to be able to understand what the bible is saying. It should be noted as well that the bible is talking about physical, spiritual, mental, financial and material strength of the people that wait on their God.

EAGLES SOAR HIGH

The eagle is a large bird of about 3 feet tall with a large wings span of about 7 feet. The large wings enable eagle to soar to an altitude of 10,000 feet or more. No other bird can be seen at that height. This is telling us that when a man waits on God he comes out excelling above others who are satisfied with their average position. An average position is an ordinary standard that most Christians want to occupy because they are not ready to pay the price. There were many prophets during the days of Elijah but none of them could rise to his level because Elijah had to do what others were not ready to do. Nothing stops everybody in a class of one thousand students from coming first. It will only mean that nobody will occupy the second position. Rising above others is a choice. But I pray that you will choose to be that Christian who will soar high above others because you are created for the top:

> **And the LORD shall make thee the head, and not the tail; and thou shalt be above only, and thou shalt not be beneath; if that thou hearken unto the commandments of the LORD thy God, which I command thee this day, to observe and to do them:**
>
> **—Deuteronomy 28:13**

It takes obedience to be blessed. When you have fully obeyed the principles of waiting on the Lord nothing stops you from soaring high.

EAGLES HAVE STRENGTH

The strength of an eagle is incomparable with that of any other bird. It has so much power to carry prey that could be heavier than its size. Just like the eagle, the strength of a Christian is an indication of how well he can do spiritually and otherwise. This is because we contend with our strength:

> **He took his brother by the heel in [their mother's] womb, and in the strength [of his manhood] he contended and had power with God.**
>
> **—Hosea 12:3 [AMP]**

Waiting on the Lord renews the strength of a Christian like the eagle to enable him soar high.

EAGLES ARE TENACIOUS

Eagles don't easily give up during hunting. The bird is so powerful that it can never surrender to the size or strength of its prey. It fights until it has overpowered its prey. A Christian that waits on the Lord will never give up until he has overcome. He persists in trusting his God no matter the situation. Just like Job, in a difficult situation, such a Christian will say:

> **Though he slay me, yet will I trust in him: but I will maintain mine own ways before him.**
>
> **—Job 13:15**

A Christian that waits on the Lord will become very tenacious like the eagles by trusting the Lord to the end.

EAGLES ARE INDEFATIGABLE

Eagles persist tirelessly when hunting for food. They can soar in the air for hours looking for prey. Many Christians easily get tired and discouraged when their answers are getting delayed. Our Lord said that ". . . **men ought always to pray, and not to faint;**"—Luke 18:1. There is a fighting spirit in the eagle bird that doesn't allow it to get tired when looking for food. This is the spirit that follows the people that wait on the Lord.

EAGLES LEVERAGE ON THE STORM

Eagle bird is so fearless during storm. When other birds fly away from the storm, an eagle spreads its mighty wings and uses the current to soar to greater heights. A Christian that waits on God will be so fearless that he cannot be easily intimidated by any challenge. Most of the time, challenges are opportunities turned upside down. All that is needed is to turn the challenge to have success. A Christian who waits on the Lord uses challenges of life to soar to greater heights. Just like Joseph when the brothers wanted to kill his dreams:

> **And Joseph said unto his brethren, Come near to me, I pray you. And they came near. And he said I am Joseph your brother, whom ye sold into Egypt.**

> **Now therefore be not grieved, nor angry with yourselves, that ye sold me hither: for God did send me before you to preserve life.**

> **And God sent me before you to preserve you a posterity in the earth, and to save your lives by a great deliverance.**

> **So now it was not you that sent me hither, but God: and he hath made me**

a father to Pharaoh, and lord of all his house, and a ruler throughout all the land of Egypt.

—Genesis 45:4-5, 7-8

His movements from the pit to Potiphar's house and then to the prison were opportunities God created to take him to his destination, the palace. A Christian who waits on the Lord cannot run away from storms of life but takes up the challenges no matter how difficult it may look.

EAGLES HAVE VISION

Eagle's eyes are specially designed for a long distance focus and clarity. It can spot another eagle soaring from 50 miles away. When the eagle bird is flying high in the sky at that height of 10,000 feet it can see little fish swimming under the water. A Christian that waits on God sees far into the future concerning God's plan for his life. The Spirit of God enables him to search the deep things of God for his life:

But as it is written, EYE HATH NOT SEEN, NOR EAR HEARD, NEITHER HAVE ENTERED INTO THE HEART OF MAN, THE THINGS WHICH GOD HATH PREPARED FOR THEM THAT LOVE HIM.

But God hath revealed them unto us by his Spirit: for the Spirit searcheth all things, yea the deep things of God.

—1 Corinthians 2:9-10

A Christian that waits on the Lord has the eye of the eagle to understand God's plan and therefore soars high above others who are walking blindly.

THEY SHALL RUN, AND NOT BE WEARY

The Christians that wait on their God shall run and not be weary.

Running in this context means the following:

(a) Making human effort:

So then it is not of him that willeth, nor of him that runneth, but of God that sheweth mercy.

—Romans 9:16

(b) To run through life especially stressful situation that comes up in life:

For by thee I have run through a troop; and by my God have I leaped over a wall.

—Psalm 18:29

(c) To make progress or go forward:

Holding forth the word of life; that I may rejoice in the day of Christ, that I have not run in vain, neither laboured in vain.

—Philippians 2:16

(d) To have growth or development:

Know ye not that they which run in a race run all, but one receiveth the prize? So run, that ye may obtain.

—1 Corinthians 9:24

We cannot live this life without making the necessary running. Our fulfillment in life depends on the progress we are making in our daily running. But those Christians who will wait on the Lord shall do it without being weary. They shall be like the eagle bird that soars in the sky for hours at a time and will never look weary. When they have run for twelve days it will look as if they have only done it for twelve minutes. This is possible when we wait on the Lord.

THEY SHALL WALK, AND NOT FAINT

The Christians that will wait on their God, they shall walk and not faint.

What does walking stands for in this context? We shall look at the meaning so that we can understand what the Lord is passing across through this statement.

Walking means the following:

(a) Our everyday life with its entire daily and often activities:

Furthermore, brethren, we beg and admonish you in [virtue of union with] the Lord Jesus, that [you follow the instructions which] you learned from us about how you ought to walk so as to please and gratify God, as indeed you are doing, [and] that you do so even more and more abundantly [attaining yet greater perfection in living this life].

—1 Thessalonians 4:1 [AMP]

Peter was exhorting the brethren in this scripture to allow their daily activities to please the Lord. These are the things we do every day to keep going in life.

(b) To go through problems or afflictions:

Though the LORD be high, yet hath he respect unto the lowly; but the proud he knoweth afar off.

Though I walk in the midst of trouble, thou wilt revive me: thou shalt stretch forth thine hand against the wrath of mine enemies, and thy right hand shall save me.

—**Psalm 138:6-7**

(c) To advance by step or make progress:

Yet I will rejoice in the Lord, I will joy in the God of my salvation.

The LORD God is my strength, and he will make my feet like hinds' feet, and he will make me to walk upon mine high places . . .

—**Habakkuk 3:18-19**

Let us consider this from the Amplified version to have more understanding:

Yet I will rejoice in the Lord; I will exult in the [victorious] God of my salvation!

The Lord God is my Strength, my personal bravery, and my invincible army; He makes my feet like hinds' feet and will make me to walk [not to stand still in terror, but to walk] and make

[spiritual] progress upon my high places
[of trouble, suffering, or responsibility]!

—Habakkuk 3:18-19 [AMP]

Walking can be concluded to mean what we go through every day or our daily routines. As we wait on the Lord while going through our daily activities, we shall walk and not faint. When we have walked for twelve days it will look as if we have only walked for twelve minutes. This is the promise of the Lord for us as we wait on Him daily, seeking His face for direction. May we walk and never faint.

CHAPTER FIVE

Hear counsel, and receive instruction,
that thou mayest be wise in thy latter
end.

—Proverbs 19:20

CONCLUSION

ONLY THE DOERS WILL BE BLESSED

Every book is a collection of instructions so that
the reader can be informed. A person who receives
information increases in knowledge to become wiser.
Reading a book becomes profitable when it blesses the
reader. And this will be possible only when the reader
applies the instructions outlined in the book.

Soaring High like Eagles is an instructional material
to bless the reader no matter your sphere of life. It is a
collection of eternal counsels put together to bless
you. The principles outlined in the book are 'biblical
principles' carefully selected out of experience. Research
has proved that most public and private enterprises that

have ever excelled built their organizations on biblical principles. And most of the inventors like Isaac Newton had religious background. Information revealed that Isaac Newton was a deeply religious person who wrote far more words on religion than he did on science. No wonder he remained the greatest scientist that ever lived.

After hearing all the counsels presented in this book, it becomes a blessing when you receive them and do them:

> **But be ye doers of the word, and not hearers only, deceiving your own selves.**
>
> **For if any be a hearer of the word, and not a doer, he is like unto a man beholding his natural face in a glass:**
>
> **For he beholdeth himself, and goeth his way, and straightway forgetteth what manner of man he was.**
>
> **But whoso looketh into the perfect law of liberty, and continueth therein, he being not a forgetful hearer, but a doer of the work, this man shall be blessed in his deed.**
>
> **—James 1:22-25**

BE WISE IN YOUR LATTER END

Latter end is the opposite of the beginning of anything. No matter what your age is today, you are at the latter end of your life. It means you are no more at the beginning of your life. You are closer to the end of your life than when you were born. Today has taken you closer than yesterday:

> **And that, knowing the time, that now it is high time to awake out of sleep: for now is our salvation nearer than when we believed.**
>
> **The night is far spent, the day is at hand . . .**
>
> **—Romans 13:11-12**

Wisdom advises you plan your end. This is the only way for you to end well. Do not allow your end to take you by surprise. Death is inevitable. It is a necessary end. It will be wise when you begin to plan for it because you have lesser time today than you had yesterday. No matter where you are, today is an opportunity for you to make your tomorrow better. You can make your latter end to be better than what you have seen so far:

> **Though thy beginning was small, yet thy latter end should greatly increase.**
>
> **—Job 8:7**

This is a prophetic word. Act on it and it will bless you.

LATTER END OF THE EAGLE BIRD

The final lap of this book is to share with you about the later end of the eagle so that you can receive wisdom to live the remaining days of your life. The bible referred to the method the eagle bird uses to renew its strength at a later stage in life to illustrate the blessing of waiting on the Lord.

An Eagle at the age of 30-50 years undergoes a harsh trial of endurance and change called **Molten Process** that last for about 150 days, according to researchers.

THE 12 STEPS OF THE MOLTING EAGLE

The following were discovered during research:

1. Over time, the beak and talons of an eagle become encrusted with calcium. Thus, they are not as sharp as they once were, and curved.
2. Their feathers become overgrown and weighed down with dirt and oil. When these things take place, it obviously hinders their ability to fly and hunt effectively. With all of the dirt and oil on its feathers, an eagle will begin to "whistle" while it is diving on its prey. With this sound coming from a bird, it makes hunting ineffective because the prey can hear them coming and have more time to run and hide before they are snatched up.

3. When an eagle gets to this point in its life, it will descend from the heights above and go to a rock below.

4. Through the molting process, the eagle begins to lose its feathers by plucking them out one by one.

5. Not only will an eagle pluck out all of its feathers, it will actually break off its beak by smashing it on a rock.

6. It will rub its talons on the rock to rub them down until they are nubbins.

7. Its vision is even said to be impaired, so their eyesight will not be as sharp as before.

8. At this point, the eagle becomes weak, vulnerable, and defenseless.

9. Many eagles die at this point in life because they cannot hunt for themselves and they can't protect themselves against predators.

10. During this time, many eagles become dependent on their companion eagles for sustenance and nourishment. They cry out and those eagles that have passed through this stage come to their aid.

11. If they can survive the shame and exposure that molting produces, then the stripping process will pave the way for the eagle to become greater and stronger than it was before.

12. It is during this time that a wonderful thing happens to those who survive. Their feathers, beak, and talons begin to grow back with greater vigor than ever before. Their beak and talons will be as sharp as ever and they will once again take to the sky. They will have acquired revitalized youth that they hadn't possessed since they were younger. And they will live for another 20-30 years.

This Molting Process is what the bible refers to as time of waiting. It's a very difficult time but it takes patience and endurance.

Once the process is over, the strength of the eagle is renewed and can mount up with wings to soar high, run and not be weary, walk and not faint. This is the portion of any person that waits on the Lord.

REFERENCE

Heart to Heart with Leif (21 April 2009). The 12 Steps of the Molten Eagle. Hearttoheartwithleif.com/?p=161